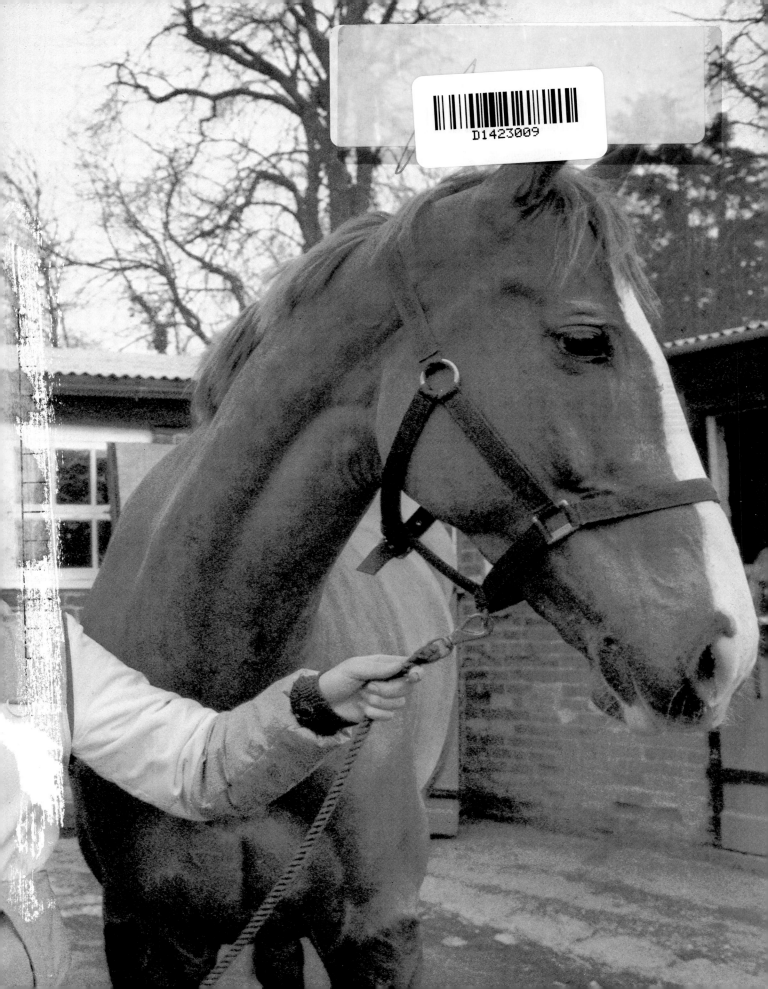

Maureen Piggott waits to take her turn in the dressage arena

Three Day Eventing
The Badminton Horse Trials

Featuring Maureen Piggott

Foreword by Lucinda Green

By Genevieve Murphy
Photographed by Eamonn McCabe

André Deutsch
105 Great Russell Street London WC1

First published in 1983 by
André Deutsch Limited
105 Great Russell Street
London WC2

Text Copyright 1983 © Genevieve Murphy
Photographs 1983 © Eamonn McCabe
Foreword 1983 © Lucinda Green

British Library Cataloguing in Publication Data
Murphy, Genevieve
   Facts about three day eventing: Badminton
   1.   Three-day event (Horsemanship)—England
   —Great Badminton (Avon)
   I.   Title
   798.2′4   SF295.7

ISBN 0-233-97528-1

Book designed by Richard Vine
Set by Alan Sutton Publishing Limited, Gloucester
Colour reproduction by
Dot Gradations Ltd.,
South Woodham Ferrers, Essex.
Printed in Great Britain by
Cambus Litho, East Kilbride, Scotland

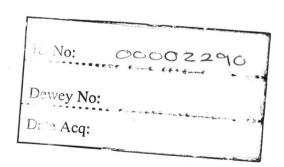

Foreword

It is with enormous delight that I write the introduction to this book, for Badminton means more to me than any other three-day event in the world.

Whenever the name is mentioned one special picture springs to mind. It is not of a huge cross-country fence or a big blue rosette, but an angled view of Badminton House peeping between the great old elms, now unhappily almost all deceased. With this imaginary sighting comes a great sense of tranquility, which is strange considering that I have been scared more times at Badminton than anywhere else. To be precise, I have been scared eleven times in eleven years.

No two people react identically. My own fear is primarily concerned with the knowledge that I may do something wrong and thereby let my horse down. By the time he arrives at Badminton, I am fairly certain that he is capable of coping with all those eye-smarting cross-country fences, provided that I do not make a mistake in my riding.

To be constantly successful in major three-day events a vital link must exist between horse and rider. The link is born from shared love and respect. It often takes several years to build, but I believe that it must exist if the partnership of horse and rider is to produce glittering results. The link enables us to tackle Badminton in a spirit of mutual confidence and trust.

In this book you will discover, as I did, many interesting facts about the other side of Badminton. Immense attention to detail is involved in every facet of its organisation. The admirable ability of its Director and his vast and selfless team, the gentle and generous support of His Grace the Duke of Beaufort combine to make Badminton what it is — the Capitol of our sport, the crescendo in which everyone involved dreams of participating.

Badminton House

BADMINTON

THREE DAYS' EVENT

THE MOST IMPORTANT
HORSE EVENT
IN GREAT BRITAIN
APRIL 20th, 21st & 22nd, 1949

1st Day—DRESSAGE, 10.30 a.m. at BADMINTON HOUSE.
2nd Day—SPEED & ENDURANCE, 14 miles, commence 2 p.m., including—
STEEPLECHASE COURSE (2 miles), DIDMARTON CAR PARK.
CROSS-COUNTRY (3 miles—21 Fences), BADMINTON CAR PARK.
3rd Day—JUMPING, 12 o'clock at BADMINTON HOUSE.
AND
TWO JUMPING COMPETITIONS (Organised by B.S.J.A.)—
TOUCH and OUT and OPEN COMPETITION.

ADMISSION to all Car Parks:
Motors, £1 per day. £2 10s., Seasons. Charabancs, £1 10s., 26 seaters.
Pedestrians 1s. each. £3, 32 seaters.
Tickets may be had in advance on payment.

CATERING BY W. OSMOND & SONS, SALISBURY

Full information from : BRITISH HORSE SOCIETY, 66 Sloane Street, London, S.W.1.

The Queen Mother with the Duke of Beaufort

Introduction

"The Most Important Horse Event in Great Britain" was born in April, 1949. The description was wildly optimistic at the time, so whoever wrote the copy for that first poster must have been gazing into a crystal ball. Before the 1949 Badminton, the organizers' sleepless nights were filled with anxiety over whether they would get a single competitor, let alone a single spectator.

The idea had been implanted in The Duke of Beaufort's mind when he watched Britain's dismal performance in the 1948 Olympic Three-Day Event that was staged at Aldershot. He had loved horses all his life, so here was a fine opportunity to attract some of the best horses in the country to his beautiful park at Badminton and let them gain experience in the all-round test of dressage, speed, endurance, cross-country and show jumping.

The first poster had to be laid out carefully so that the words "Horse Event" hit the eye immediately. Otherwise horsemen were likely to dismiss the whole thing as the game played with racquets, which was invented by the Duke's great-aunt in the front hall of Badminton House.

Twenty-two horses contested the first Badminton "Horse Event" and a good crowd turned up to watch them. The crystal ball came out again for *Horse and Hound*'s report, which forecast "it is likely to become the most important sporting event of its type."

Nowadays Badminton, the oldest and greatest annual three-day event in the World, can truly claim to be "The Most Important Horse Event in Great Britain". Over the four days it brings about 250,000 people to the county of Avon. This represents a bigger audience than any other sports meeting in the country except the Derby at Epsom. Usually, the onlookers include the most distinguished spectator in the land — Her Majesty the Queen. Riders come from all over the world, urged on by the dream of receiving the Whitbread Trophy and adding their name to the distinguished list of winners.

A vast number of people are involved in the organisation of Badminton. We will look at the parts played by the Director and course designer, by rider and horse, by television producer, secretary, press officer and others who help to make this one of the greatest sporting events of the year.

The Whitbread dray horses

What is a Three-Day Event?

Anyone who follows the sport needs to have a smart answer ready for the first Clever Dick who points to Badminton's dates and asks whether it is an Irish three-day event. It is not always easy to explain that a three-day event normally lasts for four days!

In the 1950s no explanations were needed. Less than half the present number of horses took part then, so they were all able to complete their dressage on the first day. Nowadays the dressage has to be spread over two days, adding a day to the time-table and leaving those who know with the boring task of explaining how it came to be known as a three-day event in the first place.

In common with most other three-day events, both at home and abroad, Badminton now runs from Thursday to Sunday.

Thursday and *Friday* are devoted to dressage. This is a series of movements on the flat (in other words not over jumps) which tests the horse's obedience and state of training.

Saturday is for speed, endurance and cross-country. The cross-country part is the most exciting and the only one that is normally shown on television — so it is easy to overlook the rest, unless you happen to be a competitor!

In fact, Saturday's test is divided into four sections: roads and tracks, steeplechase, more roads and tracks, cross-country. Endurance is tested by the overall length of the course (which is about 15 miles, mostly on roads and tracks). Speed is tested on the steeplechase course, and cross-country (as if you would never have guessed!) on the cross-country course.

All sections carry an "optimum time" and penalties are incurred for exceeding it. It is rare for anyone to be penalised on the roads and tracks because the speed required is not a fast one. Speed is much more critical on the steeplechase and cross-country, where you have to be very fast to escape time penalties. You also have to be accurate to avoid jumping penalties for a refusal or fall.

Sunday is for show jumping, which is the final part of this complete all-round test of horse and rider. Those who have completed the cross-country (and whose horses have passed Sunday morning's veterinary inspection) jump in the reverse order of merit.

The course is not particularly difficult, but there is still enormous pressure on the leading rider who is last to jump. As Lucinda Green said after her fourth Badminton win: "You know you can throw the whole thing away with one silly little fence knocked down."

Time-Table of Events

Wednesday, 14th April

10.00 a.m.   BRIEFING OF COMPETITORS—Badminton Village Hall
              INSPECTION OF THE COURSE
5.00 p.m.   EXAMINATION OF HORSES—North Front
                                      Badminton House

Thursday, 15th April

9.00 a.m.
approx.   DRESSAGE
6.30 p.m.   COCKTAIL PARTY—Badminton House
7.30 p.m.   Whitbread Films (Open to the public)—
& 9 p.m.   Badminton Village Hall

Friday, 16th April

9.00 a.m.
approx.   DRESSAGE
7.30 p.m.   Whitbread Films (Open to the public)—
& 9 p.m.   Badminton Village Hall

Saturday, 17th April

11.00 a.m.   SPEED AND ENDURANCE TEST
10.00 p.m.   Badminton Horse Trials Invitation Ball—Westonbirt School

Sunday, 18th April

10.00 a.m.   EXAMINATION OF HORSES—North Front
                                      Badminton House
11.00 a.m.   THREE-DAY EVENT JUMPING (if number of
                Competitors still in the Competition exceeds 20)
11.30 a.m.   Church Service—Badminton Village Church
2.00 p.m.   Dressage Display, The Band of the Welsh Guards
2.45 p.m.   PARADE OF THE THREE-DAY EVENT
                COMPETITORS
3.00 p.m.   THREE-DAY EVENT JUMPING
4.30 p.m.   Parade of the Duke of Beaufort's Hounds

Director

If you imagine that the Director of the Badminton Horse Trials sits in a plush office while others run around and do the work, you are entirely wrong. Colonel Frank Weldon does plenty of his own running around. He alone knows how every part of the vast organisation works and when people talk about him being indispensable, they really mean it. Heaven help the rest if he ever goes on "Mastermind" and makes The Badminton Horse Trials his specialist subject.

In the office, they are used to his dry wit and sharp brain. They are also used to his presence, for he puts in longer hours than anyone else. "The work never really stops and it's full belt from October to June," he says. During the full-belt period, he is up at 7 o'clock and in the office by 8.45. Lunch is a sandwich at his desk and going-home time is rarely much before 5.0 p.m. It may sound an incredibly long time to spend on an annual event that lasts for only four days, but Badminton is an extraordinarily complex event to run.

Frank Weldon has a lifetime of experience with horses behind him. Except for five years spent in prisoner-of-war camps, he has always been involved with them. They even feature in the memory of his early years in India, where he was born in 1913. He can still recall the horse-drawn carriage that was brought to the front door each day to take his father, who was a barrister, away to work.

The young Frank was about six years old when the family returned home to England and he acquired his first pony. This was in the 1920's, before the birth of the Pony Club and the introduction of junior contests. As a child, he used to hunt and compete against adults in gymkhana events for a first prize of about £1. The men were as eager for the prize money as the young lad and they did not hold back. They would have been daft

Lt.-Col. Frank Weldon

to have done so. When you ask Frank whether he was good at it, he says "not bad" in a way which implies that junior was quite capable of beating the men on level terms. Later, he became a successful point-to-point and steeplechase jockey.

"Then I went to The Shop in 1933," says Frank Weldon, referring to his early days in the army when he went to The Royal Military Academy at Woolwich, looking forward to a career spent with horses. "But as soon as I joined, they mechanised the army and took the horses away." It was not, he adds, as bad as it may sound, because an officer could get two Government Chargers, plus troop horses of slightly lower quality, and keep each of them on army forage for only fifteen shillings (the equivalent of 75p) per annum. As a result, the officers' horses became known as "fifteen-bobbers."

This "marvellous life" came to an abrupt end with the outbreak of the Second World War. Not long afterwards came capture and five long years of imprisonment. He escaped from two prisoner-of-war camps ("tunnelling was my speciality") but was recaptured and spent the last three years of the war in Colditz.

When Frank returned home as Major Weldon, he wasted little time in getting back to horses and steeplechasing. The birth of the Badminton Horse Trials came a few years later, but he was not there in 1949 to see it happen. That was the year he moved to London and became Commanding

Officer of the King's Troop Royal Horse Artillery. It was through the London job that he first heard about the new sport of eventing.

"Steeplechasing was still my first love, but I was rattling my brains to try and think of something for the young officers to do when the hunting season was over. Then somebody suggested Badminton. It had been going for a few years by then, but I had never even heard about it. I only knew about the high net and shuttlecock and racquet.

"I said we'd have a go. If you want to make anybody keen, you don't stand on the touchline and tell him to go and do it. You do it with him. So in 1952, two young officers and one foolhardy Major competed at Badminton. The boys finished the course, the Major had a crashing fall at one of the easier cross-country fences!"

The injured Major Weldon, who had cracked a bone in the back of his neck, spent a week in hospital. He regarded his fall as "bad for his morale" and resolved to do something about it. The chance came through a 5-year-old horse called Kilbarry, whom he had bought for steeplechasing. Along with the 120 troop horses at St John's Wood Barracks, Kilbarry contracted equine 'flu, but he was the only one who went wrong in the wind as a result. The "hobday" operation to improve his breathing meant that his racing days were over. He was therefore transferred to three-day eventing.

The Major's morale was restored in the Badminton of 1953, which was run as the first ever European Three-Day Event Championship. At the last moment, Frank Weldon was included in the British team — "it sounds incredible now, when you think that I had never completed a three-day event and Kilbarry had not even started in one." Incredible or not, Kilbarry finished second and the team won.

For the next three years the British team remained invincible, winning two more European Championships and the 1956 Olympic gold medal.

Frank Weldon and Kilbarry had a share in all those victories. Individually, they were second at Basle in 1954 and first at Windsor in 1955. The following year they won Badminton and went on to gain the individual Olympic bronze medal in Stockholm.

So how, you have to ask, would Kilbarry have fared at Badminton in the 1980s? The rider does not kid himself about that. "Inevitably the standard of any sport goes up. I am always reminded of Emil Zatopec, who was the oustanding long-distance runner of his day. He won three Olympic gold medals at Helsinki in 1952, but his times would not even qualify him to go to the Olympic Games now. So I can only hope that had I been eventing now I would have coped at today's standard."

Frank Weldon has played his part in pushing the standard up — as Director and course designer of Badminton, as one of the international judges at major overseas championships and as a writer, whose words appear regularly in the *Sunday Telegraph* and *Horse and Hound*. When he took over as Director in 1967, Badminton was losing money and the public was losing interest. The organisation was scattered, with the advance booking office in London, all the planning for trade stands at Gravesend in Kent and the printing of programmes and maps being done at Lewes in Sussex. The new Director changed the system and ran everything from the Badminton Horse Trials office. Since then the tide has turned and spectators have poured into the event in ever-increasing numbers.

"It's absolute purgatory," says the man who has made it happen. "Apart from the sheer numbers, the other astonishing thing is that half of them don't really know what's going on." He enjoys recounting a conversation, overheard by someone on the trade stands during the Sunday of the 1981 Badminton. Two couples had just met and one of them said, "I'm very surprised to see you here." The other replied: "Well, we heard there was a Sunday market and we thought we'd come and have a look. But do tell us, what are all those horses doing here?"

You should not take Frank Weldon too seriously when he groans about the crowds. He knows that he needs them if he is to recover the costs of staging Badminton (which now amount to more than a quarter of a million pounds) and still make the usual large profit. He has put too much in the way of hours and thought and effort into the event to be saddened by its resounding success.

Designing the Course

Frank Weldon began designing the cross-country course in 1965, two years before he became Director of Badminton. He still believes in his own long-held maxim: "The art of designing the cross-country course is to frighten the living daylights out of the riders when they see it on foot, without hurting any of the horses on the day."

He has become quite used to hearing criticisms of the course between the Wednesday (when riders inspect the fences for the first time) and Saturday (when they jump them). During this interval, riders and owners, press and public can often be heard predicting a cross-country day of disaster. Yet the designer has a remarkable talent for building new fences that look terrifying to the humans, but are taken in their stride by the horses. In 1982, Horsens Bridge (an unfinished bridge above a wide ditch) was one such example. "Believe you me, it's

No. 5 ZIG-ZAG Rails over ditch

a piece of cake," said Frank Weldon, a month before the riders were allowed to look at it. Many of the humans were horrified when they first saw the fence, yet fifty-four horses sailed over without a problem between them. The only mistakes (one refusal and one elimination) were made at the apparently much easier alternative fence.

However, Horsens Bridge, the Ski Jump and Cross Question (all brand new and alarming to look at) certainly did what the course designer intended they should do. "If you want to draw the crowds, you have to build exciting fences," says Frank Weldon. "The vast majority come to watch brave horses and riders jumping fences that they would never dream of jumping themselves. I hope everyone will gasp with horror when they see the fences, and then I hope the horses will go out and jump them without hurting themselves."

Nos. 13 & 14 VICARAGE VEE
Wide ditch followed by rails

No. 17 HORSENS BRIDGE
Unfinished bridge over wide ditch

The international rules permit a maximum height of 1.2 metres (3 ft. 11 inches) for the solid part of all cross-country fences. Hedges can be higher if the horse is able to brush through the top, but the solid part must be within the limit. The height sounds quite tame until you walk the course and see how the fences have been positioned to create extra problems. They may be close together; there may be a deep drop or yawning ditch or a drop into the lake on the landing side. They are also built as solidly as a row of houses.

Badminton's course designer is a great believer in "pinching other people's ideas and adapting them." Horsens Bridge was copied from an obstacle built for the European Championships in Denmark in 1981. The Stockholm Fence came from the 1956 Olympic Games, the Pardubice Taxis from the famous steeplechase in Czechoslovakia. Another idea he "pinched" was the Normandy Bank, which was used when the French staged the 1969 European Championships at Haras du Pin in Normandy. "While the prizes were being presented, I was out on the cross-country course taking measurements of the Normandy Bank, because I wanted to use it at Badminton."

Frank Weldon goes on to say that "while other people's ideas are helpful, inevitably most of it has to come out of my own head. Each year, from September onwards, there's a morose-looking chap in a landrover, driving slowly around Badminton Park, then stopping still and looking. That's Weldon trying to get inspiration!"

Intensive farming means that the course now has to follow the same route each year. But Frank Weldon still contrives to give it an entirely new look by changing the direction, so that the course is always jumped the opposite way round to the previous year. "That makes it far more exciting," he says. "It's dead boring if you always go the same way."

His inspirations for new fences are first drawn on paper. The designer does not attempt any fancy art-work. He simply requires a "constructional design", which he can discuss with Alan Willis,

Alan Willis (left), Gilbert Thornbury and Frank Weldon complete the Cross Question

**No. 21 SKI Jump
Tree trunk at top of steep ramp**

**Nos. 23A & B PIG-STY
Rails followed by sloping roof**

who will be responsible for building the fences. Not much more can be done on paper. "A show jumping course can be designed entirely on paper because the ground is flat," says Frank Weldon. "On a cross-country course, you have to take the contours of the ground into account." This means that he has to be out on the course to make a firm decision as to the exact place each fence will be built.

He has a few yardsticks — "for instance I know that the magic width for a step is 9 feet." So the steps at the Quarry, which horses normally jump up during alternate years are built to the magic width. Apparently this distance works out exactly right whether it is for a Pony Club event or the Olympic Games.

**No. 25 THE QUARRY
Rails and drop into quarry**

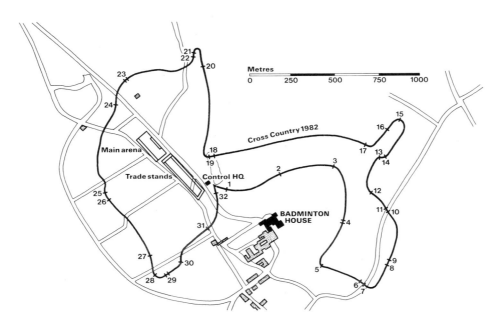

No. 26 THE QUARRY
Stone wall out of quarry

The correct distance between two fences that are close together naturally depends on the height of the obstacles to be jumped. At the Badminton heights, a "bounce" is measured at 15 feet between obstacles. This gives the horse no room for a non-jumping stride; it has to bounce straight over the next fence.

In his travels as judge and journalist, he is able to assess the standard of the competitors. About 20% of the riders will be competing at Badminton for the first time, but they will all have qualified by completing two other three-day events. The horse will have qualified (with the same or different rider) by completing one three-day event. Both horse and rider must have jumped the cross-country course in at least two contests of a specified standard (e.g. the Advanced Class at a one-day event) without incurring jumping penalties.

Frank Weldon sees all the likely entries in action at various events, both at home and abroad. With his shrewd eye he can judge their capabilities.

"People think I design the course in relation to what is coming later in the year so if the Olympic Games are coming up, they expect it to be enormous. In point of fact, I try to gauge it to the standard of the riders and horses taking part. If the standard is modest, I tend to make it easier."

Needless to say, Frank Weldon never makes it easy. Whatever the year, riders go to Badminton knowing that they will face a real challenge.

Windfall that became Fence 30

Course Builders

Alan Willis and his assistant, Gilbert Thornbury, spend the best part of six months working on the cross-country course. It is built entirely with their own two pairs of hands, plus whatever mechanical equipment they decide to use. Alan is the technical expert; he works in a spirit of mutual respect with Frank Weldon and he loves the job.

"There's always something new," he said, on the day he was putting the finishing touches to the Cross Question, one of the seven completely new fences that competitors faced in 1982.

Alan first worked at Badminton in 1966, as apprentice to George Stoneham, who was then approaching retirement. "People used to shake their heads and ask me what would happen when George Stoneham retired," says Frank Weldon. "I'd tell them there was no need to worry. I knew young Alan was dying to get his hands on the tools and do the job himself, and he's proved remarkably good at it." He points to the Cross Question, which is beautifully constructed, and adds: "You couldn't even think of designing a fence like that unless you had real craftsmen to build it."

Alan and his three brothers run a small, highly efficient firm of fencing contractors. Thanks to the reputation which Alan has established through his work at Badminton, they are now in great demand. The firm sells steeplechase fences to Sweden as well as to many of the top British trainers; in 1982 they were given the contract to build the course for a three-day event in Belgium.

Work on the Badminton course begins in the Autumn, when the bulldozers move in to Badminton Park. It is then that ditches are dug, that new banks are built and turfed. Some features, like the great mound for the Ski Jump, are created from scratch. More often the natural features of the park are modified or accentuated. For instance, there was a quarry long before the three-day event was born — but it did not look much like the multiple obstacle that horses now face on the cross-country course. Ditches are more often enlarged or scaled down than dug out of flat ground. Banks often change their outline before being returfed. By the following April they will look as though they have been shaped that way since 1660, the year when the main part of Badminton House was built.

Before constructing the fences, the course builders must select and cut the necessary timber from the Duke of Beaufort's estate. Badminton is the only three-day event in the world where timber is not ordered from a merchant and delivered in a lorry. When trees are being felled on the estate, Frank Weldon is quite liable to appear on the scene and say: "Don't you dare touch that tree! We need it for the cross-country course."

Some of the timber comes from fences that have been dismantled. Obstacles that are built in the middle of a field, like the 1982 Bull Pens, are moved as soon as the three-day event is over and the timber is stored. The drawings that appeared in the programme are all that is left of the actual obstacles. No plans are kept of the dismantled fences. Frank Weldon wants the course to be imaginative and he would never dream of rebuilding a fence so that it looked exactly the same.

Other fences, like Horsens Bridge, remain in place to be used again. With their flags and numbers removed, they blend in with the fencing and hedgerows to become part of the landscape.

Work on constructing new fences and changing old ones begins in mid-January. This is an exciting time, when Frank Weldon and Alan Willis can give full rein to their creative flair. The weather can hamper their efforts and, very occasionally, supply an unexpected bonus. In 1982, the gales blew down a tree and uprooted one of the fences. The tree was beautiful, for it had fallen with its roots intact, so that they formed a huge circle at the end of the trunk and looked like something out of Hansel and Gretel. Frank Weldon soon decided that the existing fence should be dismantled so that the tree could be used as a jump. He and Alan could not have been more delighted with their new obstacle had they blown it down themselves.

Naturally, Alan Willis and Gilbert Thornbury are in the park, with their ears flapping, on the day that the competitors first walk the cross-country course. They are understandably keen to listen to the comments. "Some of the younger riders don't know who we are," said Alan, "but a lot of the older ones do." Lucinda (Prior-Palmer) Green is among those who usually stop and talk to the course builders.

On cross-country day, Alan and Gilbert are stationed in separate places, each with a kit of tools in the back of a Land Rover, waiting to be contacted by the Army Signal Corps in case a fence needs to be repaired. If an urgent message does come, they both know the first problem will be driving to the damaged fence without mowing down the spectators.

Fortunately, they are not called upon too often. The fences are so well constructed that repairs are rarely needed.

Rider

When your father is Lester Piggott, it is not easy to slip into the world of eventing unnoticed. Maureen Piggott is not the complaining type, but she does admit that she could happily have done without the interest of the press when she first started. "Wherever I went, there seemed to be people asking questions. It's much better to be ignored when you're trying to get started, you don't want people to notice all your horrendous mistakes."

She says that her fellow competitors were not a problem in that respect. "They don't really care who you are. If they didn't worry about Princess Anne, it was hardly likely that they were going to worry about me!"

The days of horrendous mistakes were long over by 1982, when Maureen had her second ride at Badminton at the age of twenty. Like many of her fellow competitors, she had started to ride at about the same time that she learned to walk. The Piggotts still have a cine-film showing Lester leading his infant daughter on her first pony, given to her when she was only a year old.

There was no rush to replace the first pony when he was outgrown. "I went to the riding school up

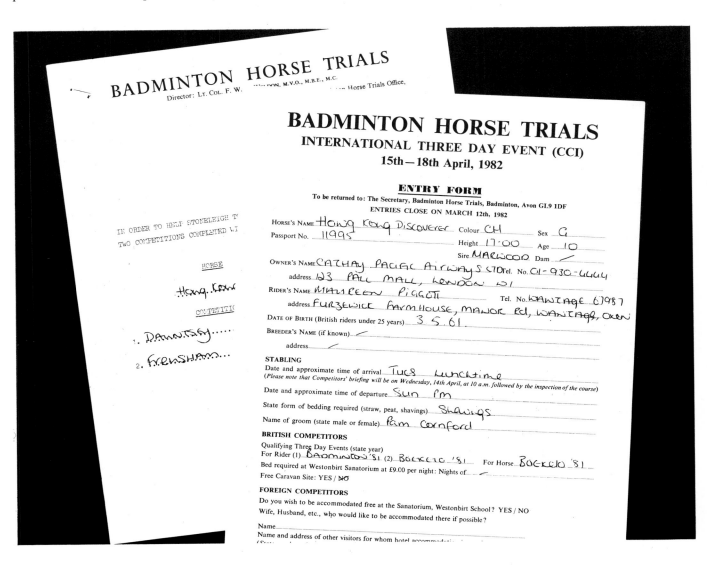

the road in Newmarket for quite a long time, before my parents were convinced that it wasn't just a passing interest," she says.

They then bought her the pony that she had been riding at the school. "He was *very* naughty," Maureen says, with great affection. "He really taught me to ride, because there was no way he would allow me just to sit on him and look pretty." The pony was passed on to her younger sister, Tracy (who is now mainly interested in racing) and the Piggotts still own him.

Maureen never had more than one pony at a time — and none of them was an angel. But they gave her the chance to enjoy a variety of horse activities, which included hunting, junior show jumping and eventing, working hunter pony and side-saddle classes. She was fifteen when she decided that she would like to take up eventing rather more seriously.

Lester Piggott nearly bought Venetia Salmond's Orpheus (who had won the unofficial Junior European Championship at Cirencester Park the previous year) for his daughter to ride. Maureen went to see Orpheus with her parents, she tried him over some of Alison Oliver's cross-country fences and found him "a super little horse." But he was then failed by the vet, Peter Scott-Dunn, because his action was not quite level.

Alison, who is one of the leading three-day event trainers, felt that Lester Piggott's daughter would have an easier start with a novice horse of whom not too much was expected. "She told my parents that there would otherwise be too much pressure from the start, too much to live up to." Having trained Princess Anne, Alison knew all about the pressures of a young rider competing under too much limelight. She therefore promised to look out for a nice young horse — and she found one in Janet Hodgson's Barney II.

Barney was only a four-year-old when Maureen tried him for the first time. "He was big and

gangly and all his bones stuck out, because he was growing faster than he could fill out, he looked like a hat-rack. He was huge and I was tiny, my legs hardly came below the saddle. But once he got going he really had something about him and we said we would definitely have him if he passed the vet. He didn't pass, because he was coughing, but we had him anyway."

Maureen saw little of the new horse for the next six months. Barney was at Alison Oliver's and she was at school, studying for "O" levels. Her parents had told her that she would not be allowed to leave school unless she passed her exams, so she worked at them with great zeal and passed in eight of her nine subjects. Then she packed her bags and moved to Alison Oliver's home in Oxfordshire.

"Alison entered me for a couple of events in the Spring of 1977, but then decided I really wasn't

Maureen Piggott with Hong Kong Discoverer

good enough to go." Maureen laughs as she tells you this, then adds: "It was fairly obvious to me as well. Barney used to tear round the place, bucking like mad. He took total advantage of me, while I adored him and felt sure that anything that went wrong must be all my fault."

Maureen eventually got the measure of the wayward horse and she was chosen for the 1979 Junior European Championship, but was forced to drop out because Barney was lame. She went on to complete three-day events at four different venues and was preparing for her first ride at Badminton in 1981, when she acquired her sponsors, Cathay Pacific Airways.

The sponsors chose a new name for Barney. He was entered in the Badminton programme as Hong Kong Flyer and became the centre of a small drama when it was discovered that the name had not been registered in time. There was a threat of disqualification before he was allowed to run under the old name of Barney that suited him so well.

Not for the first time, Barney's courage proved excessive. "He was far too brave, he'd take on things that no sensible horse would attempt. At Badminton, he found a good stride at the Quarry and then just ballooned over. Whereas other horses landed on the bank, he jumped straight into the bottom of the Quarry and had a fall. But he got straight up, carried on and made the rest feel incredibly easy."

Maureen found Badminton totally different from any other three-day event. "The distance is much longer and you really notice it — also, everywhere you go, the crowds are pressed against the ropes. Barney was completely mesmerised by all the people. I remember coming to the Normandy Bank and he was so busy gawping at the crowds that he forgot to pick his feet up to jump the rails on top." The brave Irish-bred horse somehow managed to clamber over and stay on his feet.

That was Barney's last three-day event. He contracted a mysterious illness at the end of 1981 and,

Maureen Piggott gets ready for the action

to Maureen's great grief, he died while still only a nine-year-old. Her sorrow was shared with her groom, Pam Cornford, who also loved the horse.

Meanwhile there were two other three-day event horses sponsored by Cathay Pacific and ridden by Maureen — Asian Princess and Hong Kong Discoverer. They stand at 16.3 and 17 hands respectively, which means that their saddles are a long way from the ground. When Maureen talks about the problems of falling off on a cross-country course, she is not referring so much to the way down as to getting back up again. At 5 feet 4 inches, she is smaller than most three-day event riders and, in good Piggott fashion, she rides across country with short stirrups. Getting her left foot high enough to reach the stirrup is far from easy.

The horses now live in a lovely part of the country, near Wantage in Oxfordshire, where Maureen has her own home and stables. Her parents still take a keen interest in the eventers, though her father has yet to see her competing in a three-day event. Lester Piggott was riding a couple of winners at Newbury while his daughter rode Hong Kong Discoverer round the Badminton cross-country.

Horse

Hong Kong Discoverer (1972), chestnut gelding, 17 hands, bred in Ireland. Sire: Marwood.

Owned by Cmdt. Ronnie McMahon (a former Irish international three-day event rider) and sponsored by Cathay Pacific Airways. Won the Lightweight Hunter Championship in Dublin under his former name, Parkhill.

Needless to say, the big chestnut is still known as Parkhill at home in his stable, where Hong Kong Discoverer would sound rather a mouthful. Maureen was offered the ride on him in 1980 when his owner, Ronnie McMahon, retired from eventing. Horse and owner had undergone a rough passage earlier that year in the "substitute" Olympic Three-Day Event at Fontainebleau, where they had three falls. Ronnie had been concussed in the first fall, so he was unable to be of much assistance to his brave young mount. Maureen's immediate problem was to try and restore Parkhill's confidence.

He's a very sensitive horse and he worries a lot. It took him a while to settle down after he came over from Ireland, to a totally strange place and a bunch of strange people. He was also very worried about jumping, he tended to get in a terrible panic when he came to a fence and his legs would go in all directions as he tried to get them out of the way.

"If he found himself a bit close at the second part of a combination, he'd run left instead of snapping straight up. He did that in the Sunken Road at Tidworth the first Spring I rode him and had a nasty fall. But he felt a different horse in the Autumn, when I took him to the Boekelo Three-Day Event in Holland. He was clear across country, but he went very slowly for the obvious reason that I wanted to get him round safely, as it was his first three-day event since Fontainebleau.

"By the spring of 1982 he felt full of confidence and was enjoying himself. He'd begun to pull like a train across country and my only fear was that he might go potty in the dressage at Badminton because he was so full of himself. But I knew the crowds wouldn't worry him. Having been a show horse, he loves to have people watching him and he revels in applause."

Maureen describes Hong Kong Discoverer as "a lovely stamp of horse." He is the type who would almost certainly catch her eye if she were looking for a horse to buy for three-day eventing, since he has all the qualities that she considers essential. "The horse must be put together properly and it has to be amenable, but without being dead quiet and docile, because it also has to be brave. It has to be generous too, which is why I like a horse with a nice eye and a kind outlook. It obviously helps if it moves well, though you can improve the way it moves with work."

Costs

The first major outlay is obviously the cost of the horse. A top-class eventer can fetch anything up to £30,000, perhaps even more. So those without large bank accounts or very rich and generous relatives have to go for a horse that they hope will make top-class. Even then the costs are steep. You would probably have to pay at least £2,500 for a raw novice with potential, about £10,000 for a promising intermediate and more for an advanced horse. Overseas buyers can sometimes pay staggering prices. Not long ago a five-year-old novice was sold abroad for a reputed £25,000, which is vastly more than any reasonably sane British rider would dream of paying.

The equipment for a rider who has reached the dizzy heights of Badminton is extensive and costly. There is a special saddle for the dressage, another for the cross-country and show jumping when the rider will use shorter stirrups. The bridle may be changed, the rider will need different clothes. Added to these are a whole host of smaller items — like bandages and boots, scraper and sweat rugs, breastplate and numnah.

The keep of a top-class horse is now reckoned to cost between £3,500 and £4,000 a year. Money has to be found for forage and bedding, for groom, farrier and vet, for entering the competitions and buying diesel fuel for the horsebox. No wonder so many competitors are now turning to commercial sponsors for financial help, especially as the level of prize money is relatively low.

Surprisingly, Badminton costs the competitor less than any other event. The entry fee (which was £28.75 in 1982) is not particularly cheap but, thanks to the generosity of Whitbread and Co., it covers much more than the privelege of taking part in the competition. There is free accommodation and food for the groom; free stabling, bedding and forage for the horse; a free caravan site for the rider. There are also awards for every horse that completes the competition. In 1982, these were a plaque and £50, to the owner, plus £25 to the groom. Naturally, the winner did rather better by taking the first prize of £3,000.

Training

Lester Piggott was involved in Hong Kong Discoverer's preparation for Badminton. He rode the horse each morning in his big indoor school at Newmarket while his daughter was away on a Christmas skiing holiday. "I think he enjoyed it, because he normally gets a bit bored during the winter," said Maureen.

Lester was joined by Pam Cornford, who looks after the horses. She was riding the mare Asian Princess (formerly called Grain Fair), who was also being prepared for a first attempt at Badminton. It was December, 1981, and they were already working towards the distant goal of Badminton which was four months away.

The two horses had started their preparation in mid-December. At first their exercise was limited to walking as the slow build-up of muscles began. Then they walked and trotted (with Lester and Pam aboard) in the indoor school. On New Year's Day, 1982, they moved stables when Maureen moved house and continued their training on the downs near Lambourn where the hills helped to get them fit. They had started to canter by the end of January and by early March they were cantering three times a week, up and down the surrounding slopes.

Preparations for Badminton have to cover three separate aspects of training. The horse's work must be geared so that, slowly but surely, he reaches peak fitness; he needs to be trained for dressage and ridden over fences.

Maureen does basic groundwork (in other words dressage training) two or three times a week. She works at exercises that will help the horse to be more supple and balanced in all stages of the three-day event, but the dressage is uppermost in her mind. Maureen aims to get the horse bending correctly and using the muscles in its back, so that it can perform the various movements of the dressage test with the required grace and harmony.

The horse learns to bend its back through being ridden in circles and figures-of-eight. Maureen also uses the "half-halt" to build up the horse's back muscles. This involves giving the aids to stop and then, as the horse is about to halt, pushing him forward again. The half-halt helps to pull the horse together so that its energies are controlled, like a gymnast's, and it is ready to respond to the rider. "It's important for me to get the horse together in training," said Maureen, "because the horses I ride are quite big and I'm quite small."

Her groundwork includes working through the movements in the test. So she practises such things as serpentines (a series of large loops), ten-metre circles at trot and canter, reining back (walking backwards) and the half-pass in which the horse moves diagonally. If she has a problem with any particular movement, she puts in some extra time on it. "I work at it little and often," she says. "I would never drill the horse for an hour, because it can get so bored with dressage. It is much better to limit the periods of hard work to twenty minutes and then move onto something else."

With her two Badminton prospects and a five-year old novice called Tommy Tank to school, Maureen's days were very full. She rode one horse before breakfast, the other two before lunch. She went to Alison Oliver's for weekly lessons and took part in some show jumping competitions and hunter trials, in addition to the three one-day events that she had chosen as part of the horses' preparation. She rarely schools the experienced eventers over fences at home. "I'm not particularly good at schooling across country. I ride better in a competition, even if I just go slowly round the course and use it as a school."

To get herself fit, Maureen swam, played squash three or four times a week and had the odd run up the steep hill at the back of her house — "when I could face it." There was paperwork to be done, like sending off entries and keeping the accounts. She also coped with the housework — the shopping and cooking and washing — as well as making all the curtains for her new home.

Meanwhile, the horses were building up to peak fitness and they had their first gallop in mid-March. Galloping is good for clearing the horse's wind, but again Maureen increases the work slowly. By early April, Hong Kong Discoverer was galloping twice a week, going flat out for about a mile until he was really blowing. On the day that Eamonn McCabe photographed him on the gallops, the rain was coming down so fiercely that Maureen was unable to see a thing. She was dripping soggily at the end, but still laughing.

Sadly, Asian Princess had just been withdrawn from the Badminton entries. The mare had suffered a couple of set-backs in training, first with a slight back problem and then with a cut leg. The final blow came when she broke down on her near foreleg. The vet recommended a split tendon operation, which meant that she would be out of action for the rest of the year. It was the sort of disappointment that those connected with horses know only too well.

In training at home. Maureen Piggott and Hong Kong Discoverer do some groundwork 24

Victoria Sanford (left) with Jane Gundry

Secretary

Victoria Sanford says that she became Secretary of the Badminton Horse Trials "purely by accident". Her husband, Michael, who works for the British Horse Society as the South West Regional Officer for horse trials, happened to call in the Badminton Office one day to borrow some equipment. "He asked if they needed a part-time girl for the winter," says Victoria, "and the answer was 'yes'. But there was one condition; I had to agree to take over as Secretary from Jenny Blackie when she retired the following April."

Victoria kept her part of the bargain. She took on the full responsibility of Secretary for the 1977 Three-Day Event and has been there ever since. "Every summer, I wonder whether I can do it all over again, but so far I've always come back!"

She normally comes back in early October, working two or three mornings each week in the Badminton Horse Trials office, which was once the village forge. By the middle of January she is usually working every morning and preparing for a slow build-up to the week before the event, when she works full time and flat out.

Victoria is assisted by Jane Gundry, whose father is Joint Master of the Duke of Beaufort's

Hunt and the Senior Mounted Steward during the three-day event. Jane went to the Badminton Horse Trials office straight from Secretarial College the year before Victoria and she has missed only one year since then. She now does temporary secretarial work during the Summer and Autumn, so that she is free to return to her desk in the horse trials office when required.

The office is cheerful and efficient. Everything that needs to be done is recorded in a red book that Frank Weldon calls "Victoria's bible". Both Victoria and Jane groan at the mere thought of what would happen if the building were to go up in flames, reducing the "bible" to ashes. "We would not have a hope of remembering all the things that have to be done," says Victoria.

She describes the work as varied — "a little bit of everything." Among many other duties, she produces the programme, while Jane takes charge of all the publicity material. They both work together in sending out literally thousands of car park labels to voluntary helpers, paid workers, the trade stand people and so on. The paid tickets are sent out by Joan Petre, who has run the Box Office since the 1973 Badminton and works from home. In 1982, she despatched tickets for cars and caravans and grand stand seats that were worth an overall total of £97,000.

The entries from the competitors form only a tiny proportion of the huge pile of post that arrives each day at the Badminton Horse Trials office. Those who ride at Badminton are used to filling in forms, so their entries are easy to handle.

During the actual event, Victoria and Jane move into the Secretary's tent with a mass of papers, which include 20,000 blank sheets that will be used for duplicating results. They don't see much of the competitors, who all know their way around, but they have to deal with an unending stream of enquiries from other people. "We spend cross-country day answering questions and dealing with lost children," Victoria says, with a quiet chuckle.

Assistant Director and Treasurer

Major Derrick Dyson was formerly second-in-command to Frank Weldon in the King's Troop. Now he fulfills a similar role as Assistant Director of the Badminton Three-Day Event, in which he competed during the 1950's. He is also the Treasurer and the man in charge of the avenues of trade stands, where you can buy everything from hot dogs to horse boxes.

Like everyone else in the Horse Trials Office, Derrick Dyson has been there a long time. He became assistant to his brother-in-law, Frank Weldon, before the 1971 event and is back every November to start planning the trade stand area that will stretch across Badminton Park five months later.

The brothers-in-law share the same room in the Horse Trials office, where the wall behind Derrick is virtually covered by a huge chart. This shows where every one of the trade stands, the caterers' and hospitality marquees will be located when the three-day event begins. The traders do so well at Badminton that there is a permanent waiting list containing the names of more than two hundred firms.

"We invite everyone who had a stand last time," says Derrick, "and nearly all of them want to come again. That means we are able to absorb very few from the waiting list."

Room was found for about forty extra stands in 1982 and the Rural Crafts Association had more space, which allowed sixty-six members to display their wares. This did absorb some of the waiting names, but the tented avenues are unlikley to extend any further because the Duke of Beaufort reckons that they are quite long enough already.

As Treasurer, Derrick Dyson would probably be delighted to see more firms on the waiting list accommodated. In 1982, there were 235 firms who paid a total of £90,000 for the privilege of selling their goods or entertaining their clients at Badminton and the figure would obviously go up if the number of stands increased. As Assistant Director and the man in charge of the trade stand area, on the other hand, he probably feels that he has quite enough problems with his existing clients. Too many of them park their cars and their vans in the wrong places.

Major Derrick Dyson in his office

Derrick Dyson also organises the programme sales, which are another source of revenue. 36,000 were sold in 1982, at £1 per copy. Deciding the number of programmes to print is always a tricky one and he leaves that to his Director brother-in-law. "Frank is the final arbiter. He has his ear to the ground and is able to make an intelligent guess, which usually works out right."

Badminton House

The Duke of Beaufort's butler, Leslie Vachall, is the man in charge of preparations in the beautiful house, where the Queen is a regular visitor. She always stays in the South Bedroom, which the housemaids usually refer to as the Queen's Room — until the butler teasingly pretends that he does not understand them.

Her Majesty and other members of the royal party are treated with deep respect by everyone in the house — except, one has to suspect, the parrot. The grey bird, with its flashy red tail, has a roguish way of clicking its tongue at everyone. It then says "good morning" so solemnly that you feel rude if you don't reply.

Leslie Vachall, the Duke's butler

Many visitors (myself included) have been disconcerted to hear the parrot bid them "good-bye" before they had even thought of leaving. According to the butler, the bird is a great mimic — but you don't quite like to ask whether the royal visitors are included in its repertoire.

Leslie Vachall shoulders the enormous responsibility of looking after this particular stately home with warmth and wisdom. The formality is unobtrusive. This writer only noticed it when the Duke asked: "Is Her Grace in?" and the butler replied: "No Your Grace, Her Grace is walking the dogs."

Most of the staff at Badminton House have been there for a great many years. Leslie Vachall arrived way back in 1944 and he loves the tranquility so much that he prepares for the three-day event with mixed feelings. "I cannot say that I am glad when it is all over and the Queen has left. I am deeply honoured to be able to serve her, so I could never say that. But we are used to peace at Badminton and I must admit that I am happy when it returns."

The Queen was in Canada during the 1982 Badminton, while the Queen Mother was a guest in Badminton House. Preparations for the visiting

The Duchess of Beaufort with her dog

royalty had begun, as usual, soon after Christmas with the long process of cleaning the house and all its contents. In early March, there were the usual consultations with the police over security. Leslie Vachall never asks how many policemen will be involved — but he knows some will be stationed inside the house, others will be patrolling each of the four walls, while still more will be out in the grounds with dogs.

★　★　★　★　★　★

The Duke and Duchess of Beaufort give a cocktail party in Badminton House on the first night and they invite hundreds of guests, including all the competitors. Each one is announced by Leslie Vachall and received by the Duke and Duchess. Then the guests drink champagne and talk about the horrors on the cross-country course that some of them will be facing the day after next. The butler remains with the Duke and Duchess, who undergo their own test of endurance. Having

greeted all the guests on their arrival, they bid them all farewell as they leave.

Meanwhile, Leslie Vachall has helped to prepare the menus, which have been presented to the Duchess of Beaufort for approval. The Queen and the Queen Mother have never displayed any fads or fancies about food, so the six-course dinner planned for Friday night, at the end of the dressage, is designed to please everybody. It is a long, leisurely meal that usually lasts for two hours.

On the Saturday there is a "hectic" buffet lunch during the cross-country, when important visitors arrive and depart at different times. No one needs to worry about starvation if they are in too much of a rush to eat a hearty meal. There will be another six-course dinner in the evening and a formal lunch the following day, when the Bishop of Gloucester is among the guests.

Waiting for the royal party. Choir girls at Badminton Church

Fred Viner in the B.B.C. scanner

Television Producer

Fred Viner received an urgent call from Yorkshire during the 1982 Badminton. A BBC team was in Harrogate, preparing to televise the European Song Contest, and they accused their producer at Badminton of commandeering all the available camera cable. They probably had a point. Fred and his huge team of one hundred and thirty BBC staff had helped themselves to some twenty miles of cable. They also had fifteen cameras, which was more than the budget allowed. In staff and equipment, there was the equivalent of three and a half

Outside Broadcasting Units waiting to televise the three-day event.

As Fred Viner says, "The main problem in televising Badminton is the sheer distance involved. You need fifteen cameras and all that cable if you are going to cover the whole four and a half-mile cross-country course."

Fred has been with the BBC since 1944. He joined straight from school, at the age of seventeen, as an engineer working on a transmitter in Norwich. After that, he became a film cameraman and then Chief "Sub" in the Newsroom, where he was involved in writing scripts. Finally, he became a BBC Producer in time to cover the 1964 Olympic Games in Tokyo.

In all those years, he has never allowed the job to become routine. Fred Viner carries his dedication and enormous enthusiasm to the cream of sporting fixtures in Britain. In addition to Badminton, he is the BBC Producer at such great events as the Cup Final, the Grand National and Wimbledon.

Badminton obviously requires a good deal of pre-planning. Fred Viner makes three or four trips to the course between January and the end of March and he arrives for the event itself the day before it starts. His big consignment of cameras will follow two days later — "because we elect to put all our eggs in the cross-country basket. We take a few token shots during the dressage, but our big effort is directed to the cross-country."

Expensive cameras cannot be allowed to lie idle, so they are used in other places before being transported to Badminton on Friday — just one day before the cross-country starts. They have to be set up swiftly, in positions that have already been planned.

On cross-country day, Fred Viner works for a solid five and a half hours in a huge van, known as the "scanner". He wears headphones and a mike, and he sits in front of such a complicated control panel that you wonder whether Concorde would look simple by comparison. Beyond the controls is a wall of television screens, each carrying a different picture.

The Producer has direct control of nine cameras and he can see what each of them is showing by looking at the screens in front of him. A tenth screen shows a picture from the Luckington Lane areas of the course, where the other six cameras are situated. Fortunately for Fred Viner's eyesight, these six are under separate control, so that only one picture reaches the "scanner". But there are still ten pictures for the Producer to watch. During

transmission time, he will have to keep an eye on the two extra screens that show what is appearing on BBC 1 and BBC 2.

The more transmission time Fred Viner gets, the more he enjoys his job. "That's why I'm so grateful to Princess Anne for her continued participation. The first question the editor of Grandstand usually asks me is: 'What time does Anne go?'. You can always reckon to get extra time when she's taking part."

Fred's own effort would be enough to give most of us a nervous breakdown, because so much has to be done at the same time. He listens to the commentators through the headphones; he talks to them and the cameramen through the mike; at the same time he casts an eye over those ten different pictures and selects the one to be shown. Having made his selection, he then has to press the right button on the control panel so that it is duly shown. There is no time to flick through the catalogue and look something up. He has to do his homework first, making sure that he knows the position of each camera, learning the names and order of the fences so thoroughly that he could tell them to you in his sleep.

There is no let-up for the Producer during those five and a half hours, because the BBC is responsible for the closed-circuit coverage of the entire cross-country phase. The cameramen normally work for one hour and then have half an hour off; the Producer works non-stop — "because it's too complicated to get someone to come and relieve you." He has to be ready to go "live" to Grandstand when required and to give recorded highlights to BBC 2. The following day an edited version of the cross-country phase will be shown, linking up with a "live" transmission of the final rounds of show jumping.

When you ask how he feels after five and a half hours in the Scanner on cross-country day, Fred Viner's answer is short and heartfelt. "I come out feeling bog-eyed," he says.

Press Officer

Jim Gilmore's main problem during the three-day event is in dealing with the large group of photographers that he calls the "royal chasers". He arranges one or two photo calls for them, so that they can get their picture of the Queen or the Queen Mother — and he then hopes that they will leave the royal party in peace.

It rarely works out that way, of course. Every "royal chaser" behind a camera is also looking for a scoop picture that none of the others have managed to get. One year Jim had to manhandle a French photographer out of the way. "He was sitting right inside the penalty zone, while a horse was coming to jump the fence. I literally had to drag him away."

As you may have guessed, the Queen was also at this particular fence. The French "royal chaser" was not in the least bit interested in getting a close-up of the approaching horse.

Jim Gilmore is still a working journalist on the staff of a local paper, the Wilts and Gloucester Standard. He had his first taste of journalism as a young lad during the war, when he served in the Merchant Navy and helped to produce the troops newspaper. He had his first taste of Badminton as a cub reporter, working for a local paper in Devizes, when he was sent to the inaugural three-day event in 1949. "It was my job to get the results and phone them through. At that time there were all kinds of other classes, from show jumping to working hunter ponies. I had such a terrible time chasing all the results that I thought: "I'll never come to this place again!"

But he has come back very frequently — both as a reporter and, since the 1969 event, as the Press Officer. He secured the latter job through a phone call from Frank Weldon, who had decided that one responsible press officer would be more effective than the group of Public Relations Consultants who were then looking after press arrangements. "I said I'd do it for a year and see how it went — and I've been here ever since."

Jim is responsible for feeding information to the press before the event. He mails three or four press handouts each year and is then beseiged by more than three hundred applications for press passes. During the actual event he is bombarded with enquiries that range from sensible to ridiculous. "When the Queen is here I can guarantee that at least three people will ask me what Her Majesty had for breakfast."

Major Lawrence Rook with the Ground Jury : Anton Buhler (Switzerland), General-major Rubbrecht von Butler (Germany) and Linn van der Slikke (Holland)

Countdown

Six weeks before the great event, the course builders see the first small signs of the human avalanche that will sweep into Badminton Park on cross-country day. Woodhouse and Co., the Contractors in charge of building the covered grandstands and the temporary loos, are starting to erect their scaffolding and dig their trenches. Caroline Bromley-Gardner, who does a drawing of each fence for the programme, is out in the park making sketches.

The General Stores in Badminton village is being painted ready for its busiest week of the year, when everything from tinned goods to fresh fruit and vegetables is in great demand. They are stocking up at Drewett's, the grocers and wine merchants. The village has just these two shops, plus a Post Office where they are already working flat out because they deal with all the Badminton Horse Trials mail.

About three weeks before the contest starts, the Duke of Beaufort spends a morning in the park, where he is photographed with Frank Weldon beside some of the more dramatic fences. The pictures will be sent to *Horse and Hound*, and to selected local papers, in order to get publicity and draw in the usual enormous crowds. The Duke, who was born in 1900, admits that he does slightly dread the huge invasion to come — but he studies each fence with such intense interest that you know he is looking forward to the actual competition.

He is an imposing figure, still tall and upright for the 1982 photographic session, despite a fall in Badminton House that had put him in hospital earlier that year. He said that the accident was a nuisance because it had disrupted his plans — "I very much wanted to hunt on my eighty-second birthday."

With little more than two weeks to go, television producer Fred Viner studies the course and decides where to put his cameras. The loss of a vast number of trees, through Dutch elm disease, has made his task easier by giving him more room to manoeuvre. It has also changed the landscape dramatically. A local farmer, living a mile away, says that he was unable to see the lights of a single house before the blight on the elms. Now he can see the lights of Swindon twenty-five miles away.

Ten days before the start, the peace of the sleepy village and beautiful park is thoroughly disrupted.

Jim Gilmore briefs the photographers

Schooling in Badminton Park. Captain Mark Phillips (right) on Classic Lines and Richard Meade on Speculator III

This is when the juggernaut lorries move in, bringing the parts that will be erected into large temporary buildings for the banks, where you can cash cheques from Thursday to Sunday. At about the same time, the caterers' marquees are erected and Trakway lay their great rolls of metal slats, so that traffic can move into the car parks and behind the trade stands without turning the ground into a quagmire if the weather is wet.

In the last week, it is all go. At Badminton House they are preparing for the royal party and the chauffeur is getting the Duke's Range Rover ready to carry royal passengers. The chauffeur recalls that the Queen's vehicle broke down when she was on the cross-country course in 1981, making rather a mess of their plans for conveying the royal party round the park. Fortunately there were two other vehicles travelling in convoy, so everyone piled into those. In addition to having a thorough mechanical check, the Duke's Range Rover has to be swept free of dog hairs.

Major Ronnie Dallas, who has been Stable Manager at the three-day event for sixteen years, is preparing for the arrival of the horses. He has been Secretary to the Duke of Beaufort's Hunt since the 1950s and, during the season, he still hunts four times a week. Back in 1951, he rode a borrowed hunter mare at Badminton. "I'm afraid we had a number of refusals and eventually gave up at the Coffin. If I'd known the mare longer, I like to think that we would have made a better account of ourselves."

The fine stable yard, with its sixty-two permanent loose boxes, is run by the Duke of Beaufort's stud groom, Brian Higham. It is he who ensures that a stable is prepared for each horse with the competitor's choice of bedding. Maureen Piggott has chosen shavings for Hong Kong Discoverer. She wants him to be stabled in a quiet corner, where there are few visitors to disturb him. Shavings make more of a mess in the yard than straw or peat, so they tend to be confined to the row of

temporary stabling that is tucked in behind the permanent buildings.

Back in the horse trials office, they are working feverishly. Frank Weldon presides over a Traffic Conference and, on the Sunday before the event begins, he briefs the cross-country fence judges and the timekeepers. On the day before the competition, he briefs the riders in Badminton's Village Hall.

The Director and the Ground Jury are on stage for the competitors' briefing, looking as though they are about to start acting in a play. The riders are crammed into the hall, looking like the audience for an amateur dramatic production. Frank Weldon knows his lines thoroughly. He gives details of the social events that have been

Princess Anne leaves the village hall after the competitor's briefing

organised and he explains, with the help of chalk and blackboard, how faults are incurred at the Penalty Zone — "It's all in the programme, but I know none of you read it."

There are directions as to where the riders can school over cross-country fences and where they can go for a gallop. They are also reminded that there will be a random draw to decide which horses will undergo a dope test. The riders will be told if their horse's name has come out of the hat when they finish the day's test and they must be prepared to go straight to the veterinary boxes.

Then they all spill out of the Village Hall and set off in a convoy of Land Rovers across the bumpy and often muddy roads and tracks that form Phase A of the Speed, Endurance and Cross-Country test. When they reach Phase B, the Steeplechase, they all get out to walk the 2760-metre course. They walk at an incredible rate — with Lucinda Green, four times winner of Badminton, out in front and walking fastest of all. Then it is back into convoy for the second section of Roads and Tracks, before they reach "The Box" and listen to the final part of Frank Weldon's briefing.

If they wish, they can walk the cross-country course of almost 7,000 metres immediately and find out what is in store for them. You would not blame any riders for taking smelling salts along with them when they inspect the fences for the first time. Some decide to wait until the course is less crowded, and they have lunch first, often in the Grooms' Canteen where the food is excellent. The decor is also impressive, for the canteen is in the servants' hall of Badminton House where the light of a huge open fire flickers on walls that are crowded with copper pans and stags' heads.

The riders will walk the cross-country course at least three times before they jump it. At first they want to get a general impression, next they go with the intention of deciding their exact route over each fence. The third walk round fixes the course in their minds and gives them another chance to study the alternative routes at any problem fences. Some of them will go back to study the problems a fourth time.

Princess Anne with her son, Peter

Back in the trade stands area on Wednesday afternoon, while competitors are having their first look at the course, Derrick Dyson is watching goods being unloaded. He describes this as "a crucial time, when I'm afraid I am liable to lose my temper." His problem is to ensure that everyone unloads from behind each stand, since vehicles are not allowed in front where they would ruin the grass. There are always some who make his blood boil by trying to flout this rule.

By Wednesday evening all the horses have undergone the first veterinary examination and have settled into their stables. The marquees and grandstands, the temporary loos, traffic signs and trade stands are all ready and waiting for the public to arrive. It is time for the Badminton Horse Trials to begin.

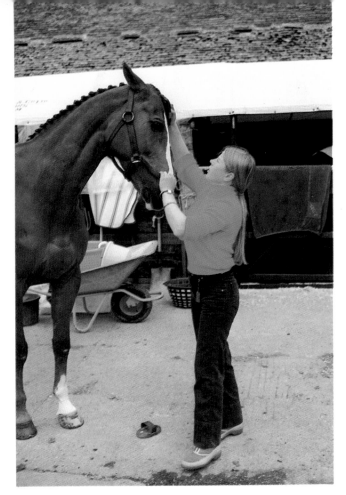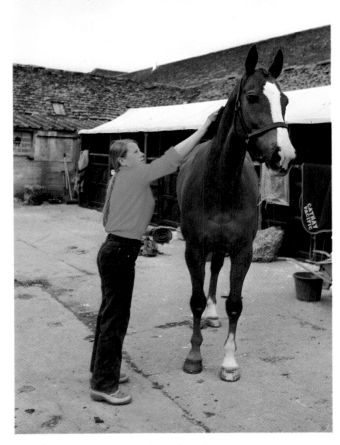

Pam Cornford allows plenty of time to get Hong Kong Discoverer ready for the dressage

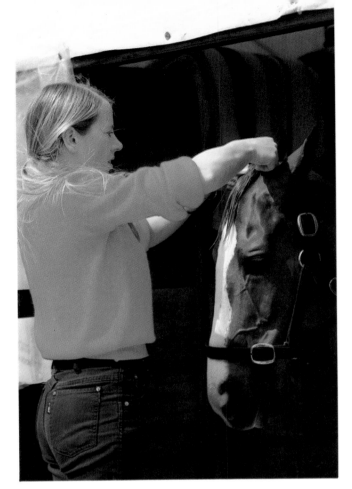

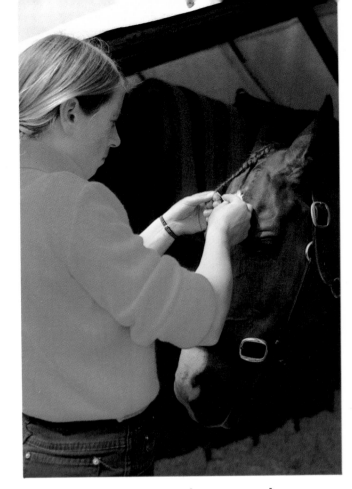

While she grooms and plaits, Maureen Piggott's Dobermann pinscher puppy keeps guard

39

Dressage

The dressage timetable lists Guinea Pig as going twenty minutes before the rest of the field. This is not a proper name. It refers to the horse and rider who go through the test simply in order to give the three judges a chance to get their eye in and mark at the same standard. In 1982 the guinea pig was Suzanne Collins, whose husband (Chris) is Chairman of the Selection Committee that picks the British team for major international championships. She had ridden at Badminton in the past and was therefore at a similar standard to many of the competitors, as the guinea pig should be.

The judges are the three members of the Ground Jury. Two of them (or sometimes all three) are from abroad and the international federation empowers them with supreme authority during the event. They have to approve the course and officiate at the two veterinary inspections, as well as judging the dressage.

They spend two whole days in separate wooden huts that look like kiosks facing the dressage arena. There are breaks for coffee, lunch and tea. Otherwise the three members of the Ground Jury are busy awarding marks out of ten for each dressage movement. These marks will be flashed immediately onto an electronic indicator for the benefit of the public and they will be noted on the score sheets by each judge's "writer".

According to the rule book, "The object of dressage is the harmonious development of the

Rachel Bayliss and Mystic Minstrel had the best dressage score for three consecutive years

physique and ability of the horse. As a result, it makes the horse calm, supple and keen, thus achieving perfect understanding with its rider."

Needless to say, it is none too easy for the average weekend rider to understand its finer points — although it must be patently obvious to everyone why Rachel Bayliss and Mystic Minstrel invariably come out on top. You don't need to be a dressage expert to recognise their superiority. The horse moves with an elastic rhythm, illustrating "harmonious development of the physique" with a finely controlled energy.

In 1982, Richard Meade finished second to Rachel in the dressage on Speculator III — whose great improvement, he claimed, was entirely due to his new German trainer, Ferdi Eilberg. Bruce Davidson from the United States was third on J.J. Babu.

Like so many other horses, Hong Kong Discoverer was bursting for a good gallop across country. He did not "go potty" in the dressage, nor did he do the best test of which he was capable. He and Maureen Piggot were lying thirty-second of the record seventy-nine starters at the end of the dressage phase.

The same pair were in the lead at the end of the dressage phase of the 1982 World Championships

Famous Riders

Lucinda Green (Great Britain)
Born 7th November, 1953
Lucinda Green, who is renowned for her verve across country, was still Miss Prior-Palmer when she gained her four victories at Badminton. She proved her remarkable ability to get the best out of any horse by winning on four different mounts — Be Fair (1973), Wide Awake (1976), George (1977) and Killaire (1979). She was also the individual winner at two European Championships (in 1975 and 1977) before she married the Australian three-day event rider, David Green. Lucinda's greatest triumph came the year after her marriage when she rode Regal Realm to win individual and team gold medals at the 1982 World Championships.

Captain Mark Phillips (Great Britain)
Born 22nd September 1948
In 1981, Mark Phillips equalled Lucinda Green's record by winning his fourth Badminton Championship. His first two successes were in 1971 and '72 with Great Ovation. Later, he was asked to ride the Queen's big grey Columbus, who had proved rather too strong for Princess Anne. Columbus gave his new rider two crashing falls at Badminton in 1973 — but he made amends with a marvellous victory in 1974, the year Mark married Princess Anne. Mark's fourth Badminton win was on Lincoln.

Bruce Davidson (U.S.A.)

Born 31st Deember, 1949

Bruce Davidson first competed at Badminton in 1974 when he came to England on an extended honeymoon with his wife, Carol. By finishing third on Irish Cap, he earned himself a place on the United States team for the World Championships later that year at Burghley. His team won and Bruce was the individual champion. Four years later, Bruce successfully defended his world title by winning in Kentucky, U.S.A., on his giant grey Might Tango. He was therefore world champion for eight years until Lucinda Green won the title in 1982.

Richard Meade (Great Britain)

Born 4th December, 1938

Richard Meade is the only three-day event rider to have won three Olympic gold medals. He was on the winning British team in 1968 in Mexico, where he rode Cornishman V through a terrible deluge that turned streams into raging torrents. Four years later, he rode Laurieston to win both individual and team gold medals in the Munich Olympics. He has won Badminton twice (in 1970 and 1982) and on both occasions he went on to ride in the winning British team at the World Championships later in the year. Richard and his wife, Angela, now live just a few miles from Badminton.

Cross-Country Day

By eight o'clock in the morning of the cross-country day the traffic is beginning to stream off the M4 at Junction 18. An army helicopter is standing by, so that the traffic police can have an aerial view of the country lanes leading to Badminton Park. If one lane becomes hopelessly clogged, the traffic can be re-routed.

The first horse is not due to start the speed, endurance and cross-country test until 11.0 a.m., but there is much to be done before the competition gets under way.

At 9.0 a.m. the six Fence Repair Teams meet in the Estate Yard. In addition to a landrover containing tools and equipment for the repair of fences, each team will be given a tractor and trailer, loaded with gravel that can be used to make good damaged take-offs and landings.

At 9.30 a.m. the Timekeepers collect their equipment from the Scorer's Tent. They have already been issued with five pages of detailed instructions and they have had an initial briefing. Frank Weldon was mistimed when riding at Badminton in 1954 (with the result that he was runner-up when he should have won) and he is determined that no such mistake will be made while he is Director.

Janet Lockhart, the official Scorer, is there to hand out the clocks and the timecards, and to explain how they work. She had been assistant Scorer for a number of years and she took overall charge for the first time in 1982. "Badminton is easier than a one-day event in the sense that you only have one thing happening per day," she says, "but it's a much greater responsibility."

Having seen the timekeepers, she allocates the jobs to her helpers and sorts out her cards. Two of the cards, prepared the night before, will provide a swift "ready reckoner" for time penalties on the steeplechase and cross-country. She will simply

have to look at the time taken and read off the penalty points beside it. She does not use an electronic calculator; the penalty points are added up in her head and double-checked.

The scores will keep flowing through from Control Headquarters, where the Director's son, George Weldon, is in charge. There will be no let-up in the Scorer's Tent, but there will be no panic either.

A variety of meetings take place at 10.0 a.m. The steeplechase judges and dismounted stewards collect at the start of the steeplechase course, the mounted stewards gather in Drier Yard, the doctors meet at the Red Cross Tent and the vets at Hound Piece, near Kennels Lodge.

At 10.15 Caroline Lowsley-Williams is ready to give final instructions to her spruce team of score collectors from the Duke of Beaufort's Hunt Branch of the Pony Club. She has been performing the same role for as long as anyone can remember — but, with only the occasional exception, the riders are all new. There is great competition to be a Pony Club "runner" at Badminton, to ride through the crowds on a smartly turned out pony while the masses walk, and they are only allowed to do it once so that others will have a chance. The team (about twelve to fourteen strong) is chosen by the six Area Managers of the Beaufort Pony Club, who each put names forward.

The riders have to be at least fourteen years of age and they must be competent. Occasionally, one of the ponies is so intoxicated by the crowds that it becomes a bucking bronco. On a few rare occasions, a rider has had to go home before the start. In 1982, one pony flew into a panic when it met up with the horse-drawn Whitbread Dray. But it recovered its presence of mind before the cross-country started, in time to perform its appointed task.

Riders and ponies are fresh and eager when they report for duty at the Box. By the end of the day they will be exhausted. Collecting score sheets from the fence judges and delivering them back to the control centre is a great responsibility and riding through huge crowds is very tiring.

Bill Thompson is in the announcer's seat on the top deck of the control bus by about 10.15 a.m. A qualified vet and course designer at the Burghley Three-Day event, he started announcing at Badminton way back in the 1950s, when he assisted Dorian Williams, and then performed the task on his own for ten years. Now he has Tom Hudson to help him — "which is much better, because the public gets bored if the same voice is shouting at them all day, and the voice that is doing the shouting gets very tired." In 1982, he did the first and last hour and a half; Tom Hudson took over for the period in between.

The Announcer's main problem (apart from the strain on his larynx) is in getting the information he needs to relay to the public. He can see only two fences, the Lake and the final Whitbread Bar, from the Control Bus. So he needs to rely on the three soldiers of the Royal Wessex Yeomanry who work with him in the bus, silently relaying the messages they receive on their radios by slotting cards into a long, narrow box on which every phase and fence is marked. If one of their three radio networks breaks down, as it sometimes does, the announcer loses touch with one section of the course.

"It's easier now that we have closed circuit television in the bus," says Bill Thompson, "but you have to be terribly careful, because the television often shows action replays. You could so easily announce that a horse had fallen for the second time, just because you happen to see the same fall twice."

★ ★ ★ ★ ★ ★

The fence judges and dismounted stewards for the cross-country have to be at their appointed fence by 10.30 a.m. Each judge's equipment includes scorebook, whistle, stopwatch, telephone,

Lucinda Green on Regal Realm

three flags and a hatchet or bill-hook for dismantling the fence in case of an accident. Like the timekeepers, they have been briefed and given a sheaf of instructions which tell them what to do under every conceivable circumstance. They will see their first horse soon after high noon, when it has finished the two sections of roads and tracks and the steeplechase.

Meanwhile, Fred Viner is in his television scanner; the photographers are stationed at fences or pursuing the royals; the reporters are out on the course or bagging a seat in front of the closed-circuit television in the Press Tent. The selectors are preparing to watch television in the Director's Tent; the Director himself is on the bottom deck of the Control Bus, waiting for the central part of the drama to begin.

Captain Mark Phillips on Classic Lines

Lucinda Green was first to go in 1982 and she made nothing of the cross-country course. Virginia Holgate jumped a marvellous round on Priceless, who seemed to be aptly named. We had to wait until the last twenty minutes of the five hours of cross-country to see the three top dressage scorers in action and, in the end, they kept the top three places. But the order was slightly different, with Richard Meade on Speculator III leading from the United States rider Bruce Davidson on Might Tango and Rachel Bayliss on Mystic Minstrel.

Ireland's Siobhan Reeves-Smith . . .

takes an unscheduled bath at the lake

She remounted and finished the course

Rider's Day

The 1982 cross-country day began early for Maureen Piggott, who was staying in a caravan provided by her sponsors, Cathay Pacific Airways. She was up at six o'clock, anxious to have a third and final walk around the four and a half-mile cross-country course before breakfast.

"I went to walk the course early, because I thought I'd miss all the people — but there seemed to be about 100,000 French walking around in large groups. It wasn't too bad, you could see the fences, but I was amazed to find so many people out and about at that hour. As I was just walking from fence to fence, it only took me about an hour and a quarter. I suppose it must have taken me twice as long the previous day, when I was working out which way I would go."

Maureen then had breakfast in the caravan before going to see Hong Kong Discoverer. Pam would be leading the horse out for a short while that morning, but he would not be ridden until it was time to start in the competition. The roads and tracks on Phase A would give him plenty of chance to loosen up.

Next, Maureen went in search of Alison Oliver because she wanted her advice about riding the Vicarage Vee, which she planned to jump across the corner. It would save her about ten seconds (the equivalent of four penalty points), but she needed to get her line exactly right. The rider and trainer walked back to the Vicarage Vee and decided on the best line, then selected a distant tree that would guide Maureen along the right path. After that, the rider weighed out — with saddle and bridle and the necessary pieces of lead that would bring the weight up to the required minimum of 75 kg. (11 stone 11 lbs.).

Maureen then went to watch the start of the competition on closed-circuit television. Obviously, it helps to watch others tackling the course and see how the various fences are riding. "I still wasn't too sure about Horsens Bridge and was considering jumping the alternative. But everyone I saw jumped the Bridge, and they jumped it very well. I also saw plenty of horses taking the corner of Vicarage Vee very comfortably. I didn't see any terrible mistakes, just some minor ones and you can learn by them."

At about 1.30 p.m., feeling reasonably encouraged after her time in front of the television, Maureen went back to the stables and bandaged Hong Kong Discoverer. Pam saddled the horse, Maureen mounted and rode to the start in the front of Badminton House, ready to set off at the appointed hour of 3.24 p.m.

The starter gave her the usual warnings: "One minute to go . . . thirty seconds to go . . ." Then they were off at a brisk trot, which they maintained for the whole of the first section of roads and tracks. "We were quite early into the start of the steeplechase, which is no bad thing. When the horses know what they are doing, they often take quite a hold on Phase A and it wastes energy fighting them." So Maureen let the eager Hong Kong Discoverer trot at his own speed instead of trying to restrain him.

She was delighted by the way he went on Phase B, the steeplechase. "The previous autumn, in Holland, he wasn't too sure about his steeplechasing and there was a touch and go feel about it. But he went really well at Badminton and was much quicker to recover than he had been in Holland."

Maureen walked for the first kilometre of Phase C (the second section of roads and tracks) to give the horse a chance to get his breath back. That meant she had to trot the remaining 8.9 kilometres to finish within the time. "The worst part of Phase C is when you come back into Badminton Park and are confronted by millions of people. It all looks dead simple when you're driven round the roads and tracks, you don't anticipate any problem

in seeing your way to the finish. Fortunately they have two huntsmen to lead you through — otherwise you wouldn't know where to go, you'd be totally lost in the crowds."

Hong Kong Discoverer then trotted into the spacious enclosure, known as "The Box", and he passed the vets' examination without any problem. Maureen does not believe in taking the saddle off during the compulsory ten minute halt at the end of Phase C — "because the horse is then inclined to think he has finished for the day. It means leaving a wet numnah on his back — but it's warm and wet, and you know it won't have time to get cold, so it doesn't really matter. We try to avoid doing too much at this stage, because it can become an awful rush and you need to give the horse a chance to relax."

Alan Oliver (show jumping husband of Alison) held Hong Kong Discoverer while Pam sponged him over. Then Pam checked shoes and studs, bandages and over-reach boots. There was time for a quiet walk round before she greased the horse's legs, ready for the "off". If he hit a fence, the grease would help him to slide his limbs over without scraping them.

Meanwhile, Maureen was talking to Louise Bates and Janet Hodgson. Both had completed the course and were generous and helpful with their advice. Then the rider sat down for a little while and started to worry. "I'm never anxious or nervous at any other stage in a three-day event, it's only during those ten minutes in the Box that I start thinking about the cross-country fences and worry about the way I'm going to ride them. The corner of the Vicarage Vee still loomed large in my thoughts, I had to be sure that I took the right line to it."

Soon she was back up on Hong Kong Discoverer and listening to the countdown for the start of Phase D, the cross-country. Then she set off in a hurry. "I planned to be quite quick, so we went away very fast and really attacked the first three fences." There was a loud clang as the horse hit the Whitbread Barrels, the first fence on the course, but he touched very little else.

Maureen Piggott riding across country on Hong Kong Discoverer

Maureen was momentarily confused as she jumped on the far left of the Zig-Zag at Fence 5, because she had expected that the little orange pegs which marked the penalty zone would be removed. Instead she had to find a path through them. Hong Kong Discoverer was still going well when he came to the Vicarage Vee (fences 13 and 14), where Maureen lined herself up with her chosen tree in the distance. "Janet had told me not to look for a stride, she said I just needed to kick on. So I stared fixedly at the tree and kept kicking!" The horse jumped easily over the corner, where the two fences could be taken in one leap.

He also flew over Horsens Bridge (fence 17), went neatly through the lake (18 and 19) bounced easily off the Normandy Bank (20) and made nothing of the Ski Jump (21). "That was the last of five

drop fences in a row, which was not very kind on the horse." Maureen would have jumped six consecutive drop fences, where the landing was lower than the take-off, had she not taken the alternative route at the 15th because she disliked the look of the Stockholm Fence. A succession of drops is never popular, because it can jar the horses — especially if the ground is on the firm side, as it was in 1982.

The Pig-Sty at fence 23 gave Maureen a fright. Being Irish, Hong Kong Discoverer is used to jumping banks and he tends to put his feet down on any fence that looks solid. He banked the Pig-Sty, landed very steeply, took one stride and then almost toppled over. Maureen felt sure that he would fall, but she sat tight while he somehow managed to find his feet — "which was very clever

49

of him." The experience did not upset the horse. He jumped the next fence, the Keeper's Rails, with easy fluency.

Then they came to The Quarry (fences 25 and 26). "He jumped the first part beautifully, but too boldly," says Maureen, with a quiet chuckle. "Then he went sailing down the ramp and straight out of the penalty zone at the bottom." She didn't realise the mistake at the time, so it was a big disappointment to discover that she had incurred 20 penalties for leaving the penalty zone before jumping out of The Quarry.

The last six of the 32 fences were cleared easily and Hong Kong Discoverer was still full of running at the finish. Then Pam took the horse, while Maureen weighed in and was interviewed for television by Raymond Brooks-Ward — "which is not the easiest thing to have happen, when you are still puffing and panting."

She returned to The Box, feeling quited pleased with herself, to find everybody looking thoroughly miserable. Her mother and Alison Oliver, the McMahons (who own Hong Kong Discoverer) and her sponsors from Cathay Pacific Airways were all full of gloom. "I couldn't understand what was wrong. Then I heard that the horse had walked away terribly lame and they all thought he had broken down."

Happily, they were wrong. Maureen believes that he must have been very stiff — "Like a person who has run a long way, then stopped still for a minute or two and begun to feel shaky when moving off again." When she went to look at him in the stables, there was not a mark on his legs and he was as sound as a bell. She and Pam washed Hong Kong Discoverer down and walked him round for a while to ease the stiffness. By the time they had finished, it was 8 o'clock. Maureen was dog tired and her back, which gives her a fair bit of trouble, was aching painfully.

But the big Irish chestnut was fit and well. He had finished just 1.6 seconds outside the optimum time and was lying in twenty-third place. But for those unlucky twenty penalties at The Quarry, he would have been eleventh of the seventy four who started on the cross-country.

The end of a long day

Maureen Piggott leads Hong Kong Discoverer out for the veterinary inspection

Show Jumping

The first important test on show jumping day is the one which takes place in the morning, in front of the Ground Jury and the vets. Each horse has to be passed fit and sound before it is allowed to continue in the competition.

A large crowd is there to watch the horses being walked and trotted in front of Badminton House. There is disappointment, especially among the "royal chasers" in the press corps, when it is learnt that the Queen Mother has caught a chill and will not be attending the veterinary inspection. While the vets are inspecting, a figure appears dimly at an upstairs window. "It's the Queen Mum," says one royal chaser, and the telephoto lenses swing into action so rapidly that some of us are in danger of decapitation.

In the afternoon, a parade of competitors precedes the show jumping. The object of this final phase is "to prove that, on the day after a severe test of endurance, the horses have retained the suppleness, energy and obedience necessary for them to continue in service." On its own it would not be exciting. It is only fraught with tension because so much is at stake; what has been gained in the dressage and on the dramatic cross-country roundabout can so easily be lost on the much tamer show jumping swings.

They jump in the reverse order of merit, which puts extra pressure on the leader — especially when he has less than five penalties (the cost of one knocked down fence) in hand. In 1982, Richard Meade had only 1.8 penalties in hand from America's Bruce Davidson.

On the press seats, we were all remembering the climax of the 1972 Badminton, when Richard

Marching display before the start of the show jumping

The Queen Mother arrives

threw away his fractional advantage over Mark Phillips by jumping his safe clear round too slowly and incurring time penalties, which dropped him to second place. "You don't make that mistake twice," he said, rather sharply, when we reminded him of it later.

Despite the pressure, Richard succeeded in jumping a relaxed and fluent clear round that was well within the time allowed. The cheers rang out as the great all-round test of horses and horsemanship ended with a win for Richard Meade, with Bruce Davidson second and Rachel Bayliss third. Maureen Piggott had one fence down on Hong Kong Discoverer, but still moved up six places to finish seventeenth.

The winner, who lives so close to Badminton that he had hacked Speculator III to the event, still had plenty to do. First came the joy of the

Maureen Piggott in the show jumping arena with Hong Kong Discoverer

The Queen Mother and Richard Meade

presentation when he received the Whitbread Trophy from the Queen Mother. Then he was interviewed for television, photographed by the cameramen who formed a shutter-clicking semi-circle around him and the horse, and finally interrogated by the press.

The polished forty-three year-old horseman took it all in his stride. When asked about Speculator, the veteran fourteen-year-old sponsored by George Wimpey and Sons, he tended to repeat one favour-ite line: "He's a very exciting horse to ride." Apparently, he was once rather too exciting. "When I first rode him, I thought he was a dangerous horse. It felt as though he shut his eyes when he came to a fence. Only the rider is allowed to do that!"

Finance

It cost about £300,000 to stage the 1982 Badminton and the three-day event still made a thumping profit of £90,000. The biggest items on the expense side of the balance sheet included:

Building the cross-country course — £15,000
Temporary grandstands — £26,000
Temporary loos (with seating for 800!) — £12,000
Printing of programmes — £12,000
Salaries and wages — £28,000
Insurance — £7,500

The insurance is essential in case the event has to be cancelled through bad weather. Needless to say, it is never called off just because it happens to be raining. Badminton has been cancelled only three times in twenty-four years and on each occasion it had been raining for so long that the ground was a quagmire. If the event has to be abandoned at the last moment, the insurance will cover a substantial part of the expenses — but it won't cover them all.

The income in 1982 was about £390,000. The biggest item of revenue was admission to Badminton Park. About a quarter of a million people paid a total of £150,000 to drive their cars into the park, or to walk in on foot and watch the three-day event. They bought 36,000 programmes at £1 each and they paid another £37,000 for reserved seats in the grandstand. The trade stands and hospitality marquees produced an income of £90,000.

All this was good news for the British Horse Society that reaps the benefits. In 1982, the B.H.S. received a nice fat cheque for £86,000 to help in its work of looking after horse interests, including training and welfare. The remainder of the £90,000 profit stayed in the Badminton Horse Trials account so that work could commence on the 1983 Championship.

Aftermath

"The day after Badminton is always horribly flat," says Victoria Sanford. "We come into the office on the Monday to find the phone doesn't ring any more. All that's left is the clearing up."

Out in Badminton Park the clearing up involves picking up tons of litter. Local boy scouts have been collecting it during the event. On the Monday, local school children take over. A machine is also used; it is pulled by a tractor and it sucks up litter like a vacuum cleaner.

In the office, Victoria's "bible" reminds her that thank-you letters must be sent to all those who helped. Results and a copy of the programme must go to the Federation Equestré Internationale and

Keeping Britain tidy

Helping to clear the tons of rubbish

the National Federations of all the countries that competed. A plaque has to be sent to the breeder of the winning horse (if known). Invitations to the Village Party must be dispatched ("remember Post Office and postmen") and the dates for next year's

event sent to a long list of people. Jane stays on for a week to help Victoria with the clearing-up.

Frank Weldon is still working hard, tying up the ends of the Badminton that is just over and laying the foundations of the next one. Derrick Dyson is wrestling with the figures for the balance sheet that will have to be ready for the auditors in early June.

Hong Kong Discoverer is making "a general nuisance" of himself at home. He has regained his appetite for jumping fences and proves the point by jumping out of his paddock on five occasions. "We dare not turn him out again," says Maureen Piggott, "because he's too precious. We can't take the risk of him damaging himself." So the horse is led out of his stable for a walk each day while a higher fence is being built around the smallest paddock.

When all the office work is done, Derrick concentrates on insurance broking, Victoria tends her "enormous garden" and Jane does temporary secretarial work. The deer return to their peaceful grazing in Badminton Park and the spring grass grows quickly through the imprints of half a million boots and hundreds of horseshoes.

Frank Weldon is once again free to think of some more ingenous ways of "frightening the living daylights out of the riders."

Records

Past winners of the Badminton Championship

1949 John Shedden (G.B.) on Golden Willow

1950 Capt Tony Collings (G.B.) on Remus

1951 Capt Hans Schwarzenbach (Switzerland) on Vae Victus

1952 Capt Mark Darley (G.B.) on Emily Little

1953 European Championship. Major Lawrence Rook (G.B.) on Starlight

1954 Margaret Hough (G.B.) on Bambi V

1955 Moved to Windsor for European Championship. Major Frank Weldon (G.B.) on Kilbarry

1956 Major Frank Weldon (G.B.) on Kilbarry

1957 Sheila Willcox (G.B.) on High and Mighty

1958 Sheila Willcox (G.B.) on High and Mighty

1959 Sheila Waddington (née Willcox, G.B.) on Airs and Graces

1960 Bill Roycroft (Australia) on Our Solo

1961 Laurie Morgan (Australia) on Salad Days

1962 Anneli Drummond-Hay (G.B.) on Merely-a-Monarch

1963 Cancelled

1964 Capt James Templer (G.B.) on M'Lord Connolly

1965 Major Eddie Boylan (Ireland) on Durlas Eile

1966 Cancelled

1967 Celia Ross-Taylor (G.B.) on Jonathan

1968 Jane Bullen (G.B.) on Our Nobby

1969 Richard Walker (G.B.) on Pasha

1970 Richard Meade (G.B.) on The Poacher

1971 Lt Mark Phillips (G.B.) on Great Ovation

1972 Lt Mark Phillips (G.B.) on Great Ovation

1973 Lucinda Prior-Palmer (G.B.) on Be Fair

1974 Capt Mark Phillips (G.B.) on Colombus

1975 Cancelled

1976 Lucinda Prior-Palmer (G.B.) on Wide Awake

1977 Lucinda Prior-Palmer (G.B.) on George

1978 Jane Holderness-Roddam (née Bullen, G.B.) on Warrior

1979 Lucinda Prior-Palmer (G.B.) on Killaire

1980 Mark Todd (New Zealand) on Southern Comfort

1981 Capt Mark Phillips (G.B.) on Lincoln

1982 Richard Meade (G.B.) on Speculator III

Glossary

Aids
Signals given by the rider's hands, legs and weight of the body. They tell the horse what the rider wishes him to do.

Bank
When a horse puts its feet onto a fence, as though jumping onto a bank.

Bounce
A horse is said to bounce when it jumps two fences that are so close together there is no room for a non-jumping stride between them.

Box, The
An enclosure where riders weigh out before the start of the speed, endurance and cross-country test, and weigh in at the finish. The Box is also the place where riders and horses have a compulsory ten-minute break before the cross-country. During that time each horse is examined by a panel of experts, who decide whether it is fit enough to continue.

Burghley
The Burghley Three-Day Event is the major contest of the Autumn season in Britain. It is held on the Burghley House estate, which adjoins the Lincolnshire town of Stamford. Two World Championships have been staged there (in 1966 and 1974).

Cross-country
The most important section of the speed, endurance and cross-country test. It is the part that includes all the most difficult fences.

Dressage
A series of movements performed at walk, trot and canter. Each movement is marked individually by the three judges; points are also given for the overall impression. The scorers then find the average of the three judges marks. They deduct this from the maximum number of points that can be awarded to give a penalty score. This score is multiplied by the "multiplying factor" to give the actual number of penalty points that the horse will carry through to the next phase.

Drop fence
A fence where the landing is lower than the take-off.

Examination of horses
All horses have to pass a veterinary inspection before the start of a three-day event. They are inspected again before the start of the cross-country and on the morning of the final show jumping.

F.E.I.
Federation Equestré Internationale. The ruling body for all equestrian sports except racing.

Grading
There are three grades for event horses in Britain: I (advanced), II (intermediate) and III (novice). Horses are upgraded through points gained at the British Horse Society's official horse trials.

Hands	Used in measuring the height of a horse from its withers (which are just in front of the saddle) to the ground. One hand is equal to 4 inches (10.2 cm).
Horse Trials	A term that covers all eventing competitions, including one-day events.
International Championships	In addition to the Olympic Three-Day Event, there are World Championships (held every 4 years) and European Championships (held every 2 years). This means that there is a major international championship every year. There are also annual European Championships for juniors (16–18 years of age) and young riders (19–21).
Level	When a horse is level it moves with an even gait. The horse that is not level avoids putting its weight evenly on all 4 legs. This may be caused by stiffness, or it may mean some more serious problem.
Multiplying factor	The means by which the dressage phase is made to have the correct influence on the whole competition. It varies between ½ and 1½. The actual figure will depend on the severity of the cross-country course — the harder it is, the higher the multiplying factor.
Numnah	A sheepskin pad used under the saddle, which absorbs sweat and helps to protect the horse's back from saddle sores.
Optimum time	The time allowed for each section of the speed, endurance and cross-country phase. It is calculated on the distances and the speed required for each section. Penalties are incurred for exceeding the optimum time.
One-day event	A contracted form of three-day eventing in which dressage, cross-country and show jumping are ridden on the same day.
Over-reach boots	Protective covering that prevents injuries caused by the toe of a hind foot striking into the heel of a fore foot.
Penalty zone	An area surrounding steeplechase and cross-country fences. It extends 10 metres before and 20 metres beyond each fence, at a width of 10 metres from the flags on each side of the obstacle. In multiple obstacles (where two or more fences are close together) the penalty zone is continuous. Leaving the zone without jumping all the fences in a multiple obstacle is penalised as a refusal. Falls outside the penalty zone are not penalised except by loss of time.
Refusal	A horse is said to refuse when it stops in front of a fence and to have run-out when it swerves past the obstacle. Both forms of disobedience are penalised the same way.
Roads and tracks	These test the horse's stamina during the speed, endurance and cross-country. The roads and tracks are normally on a private estate and they have to be covered at a speed of 220 metres per minute.

Scoring

The horse with the lowest total of penalty points at the end of the competition is the winner. In the case of equality, the horse that is closer to the optimum time across country is awarded the higher placing. Methods of scoring for each phase are given under their separate headings — i.e. (1) dressage, (2) speed, endurance and cross-country and (3) show jumping.

Show jumping

The final phase of a three-day event in which penalties are incurred as follows:
Fence knocked down: 5 penalties
One or more feet in the water: 5 penalties
Refusals (including running out or circling) First: 10 penalties; second: 20 penalties; third: elimination
Fall of horse and/or rider: 30 penalties
Each second over the time allowed: ¼ penalty
Exceeding the time limit or taking the wrong course: elimination

Speed, endurance and cross-country

A test consisting of four separate sections: (A) and (C) roads and tracks, (B) steeplechase and (D) cross-country. Time penalties can be incurred on all four sections, though it is rare for anyone to exceed the optimum time on the roads and tracks. For each second over the optimum time competitors incur 0.8 of a penalty on the steeplechase and 0.4 on the cross-country. Jumping penalties on the steeplechase and cross-country course are incurred as follows:
Refusals (including running-out or circling). First: 20 penalties; second (at the same obstacle): 40 penalties; third (at the same obstacle): elimination
Fall of horse and/or rider: 60 penalties
Second fall on steeplechase: elimination
Third fall on cross country: elimination
Taking the wrong course: elimination

Take hold

When a horse takes the bit strongly, pulling against its rider in its eagerness to go fast.

Team competitions

The Olympic Games and the World and European Championships offer team as well as individual awards. Each team consists of three or four riders, with only the best three scores counting towards the team total.

Weights

There is no minimum weight for the dressage. In the other two phases horses are required to carry a minimum of 75 kg (11st 11 lb). Lead weights must be carried if the combined weight of rider and saddle is less than the minimum.

**Maureen Piggott galloping
Hong Kong Discoverer
in the rain**